Sara Swan Miller

Wading Birds

From Herons to Hammerkops

Franklin Watts - A Division of Grolier Publishing
New York • London • Hong Kong • Sydney • Danbury, Connecticut

Photographs ©: BBC Natural History Unit: 7 bottom (Jeff Foott), 23 (Hans Christoph Kappel), 43 (Tom Vezo), 27 (Adam White), 7 top (Mike Wilkes); Corbis-Bettmann: 42; Dembinsky Photo Assoc.: 17 (Tom Boyden), 29 (Stan Osolinski), 15 (Jim Roetzel), 21, 41 (Mark J. Thomas); Peter Arnold Inc.: 1 (Fred Bruemmer), 5 bottom left (S. J. Krasemann), 5 bottom right (John R. MacGregor), 6 (Albert Visage); Photo Researchers: cover (Harry Engels), 5 top right (Tom McHugh), 5 top left (Rod Planck), 36, 37 (Sandy Sprunt); Tony Stone Images: 19 (Leonard Lee Rue III), 33 (Reinhard Siegel); Visuals Unlimited: 31 (Barbara Gerlach), 35 (Ken Lucas), 39 (Joe McDonald), 25 (Milton H. Tierney, Jr.), 13 (Gustav W. Verderber).

Illustrations by Jose Gonzales and Steve Savage

The photo on the cover shows a black-crowned night heron. The photo on the title page shows two flamingos.

Visit Franklin Watts on the Internet at:
http://publishing.grolier.com

Library of Congress Cataloging-in-Publication Data

Miller, Sara Swan.
Wading birds: from herons to hammerkops / Sara Swan Miller.
     p. cm. — (Animals in order)
   Includes bibliographical references and index.
   Summary: Describes the general characteristics of wading birds and the specific physical traits and behaviors of fifteen species, including herons, bitterns, ibises, storks, egrets, and flamingos.
   ISBN 0-531-11630-1 (lib. bdg.)   0-531-13959-X (pbk.)
   1. Ciconiiformes—Juvenile literature. [1. Wading birds. 2. Birds.] I. Title. II. Series.
QL696.C5 M56   2001
598.3'4—dc21   99-0575359

Contents

A Look at Wading Birds

Have you ever seen a great blue heron standing tall and still along the edge of a pond? Have you ever watched a flamingo wade slowly through a marsh, swinging its curved bill through the water? Maybe you have seen a flock of ibises walk at the edge of a lagoon, poking in the mud with their sharp, curved bills. You might have watched cattle egrets strutting across a field behind a herd of cows.

Did you know that all these birds are closely related? They belong to a group, or *order*, of birds called the ciconiiformes (sih-kon-ih-ih-FOR-meez). Most people call them wading birds. On the next page, you can see pictures of four kinds of wading birds. Can you guess why scientists group them together?

Great blue heron

Whale-headed shoebill

Roseate spoonbill

Greater flamingo

Traits of the Wading Birds

Wading birds have long thin legs, broad wings, and a short tail. Their long legs keep their feathers dry as they wade in shallow water. Since most wading birds have large bodies, they need broad wings to fly.

Like other wading birds, this scarlet ibis has thin legs, broad wings, and a short tail.

One thing that makes it easy to tell one wading bird from another is its bill. Some wading birds use their long, pointed bill to catch fish. A spoonbill uses its bill to pick up floating *prey*. A flamingo uses its bill to strain small animals out of the water. Boat-billed herons and

A goliath heron eats lots of fish.

shoebills have large, flat, strong bills that are good for scooping up prey.

All wading birds eat small animals. Most eat fish, but some also eat frogs, tadpoles, eels, insects, crabs, shrimp, snails, worms, or mussels. Many eat the eggs and young of smaller birds. A few eat small mammals, such as a mouselike creature called a vole.

Unlike other waterbirds, most wading birds do not have webbed feet. That's because most wading birds don't swim. Webbed toes would just get in the way as they wade in shallow waters or stalk through fields. A few kinds of wading birds have a little webbing between their toes, but only flamingos have fully webbed feet.

Wading birds often nest with other members of their species in large, noisy *colonies*. The young are helpless when they hatch. Their parents feed them until they are ready to fly.

A mother great egret with her chick

The Order of Living Things

A tiger has more in common with a house cat than with a daisy. A true bug is more like a butterfly than a jellyfish. Scientists arrange living things into groups based on how they look and how they act. A tiger and a house cat belong to the same group, but a daisy belongs to a different group.

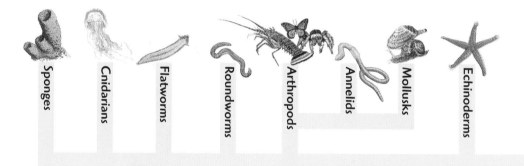

Sponges Cnidarians Flatworms Roundworms Arthropods Annelids Mollusks Echinoderms

Animals

Plants Fungi

Protists

Monerans

All living things can be placed in one of five groups called *kingdoms*: the plant kingdom, the animal kingdom, the fungus kingdom, the moneran kingdom, or the protist kingdom. You can probably name many of the creatures in the plant and animal kingdoms. The fungus kingdom includes mushrooms, yeasts, and molds. The moneran and protist kingdoms contain thousands of living things that are too small to see without a microscope.

8

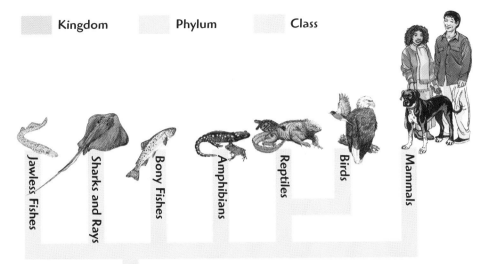

Kingdom   Phylum   Class

Jawless Fishes
Sharks and Rays
Bony Fishes
Amphibians
Reptiles
Birds
Mammals
Chordates

Because there are millions and millions of living things on Earth, some of the members of one kingdom may not seem all that similar. The animal kingdom includes creatures as different as tarantulas and trout, jellyfish and jaguars, salamanders and sparrows, elephants and earthworms.

To show that an elephant is more like a jaguar than an earthworm, scientists further separate the creatures in each kingdom into more specific groups. The animal kingdom can be divided into nine *phyla*. Humans belong to the chordate phylum. Almost all chordates have a backbone.

Each phylum can be subdivided into many *classes*. Humans, mice, and elephants all belong to the mammal class. Each class can be further divided into orders; orders into *families*, families into *genera*, and genera into *species*. All the members of a species are very similar.

How Wading Birds Fit In

You can probably guess that wading birds belong to the animal kingdom. They have much more in common with spiders and snakes than with maple trees and morning glories.

Wading birds are members of the chordate phylum. Almost all chordates have a backbone and a skeleton. Can you think of other chordates? Examples include elephants, mice, snakes, frogs, fish, whales, and humans.

All birds belong to the same class. There are about thirty orders of birds. Wading birds make up one of these orders.

Scientists divide wading birds into a number of different families and genera. There are 140 species of wading birds. Wading birds live in almost every part of the world. They live in fields and wetlands and along the shores of ponds, lakes, rivers, and streams. In this book, you will learn more about fifteen species of wading birds.

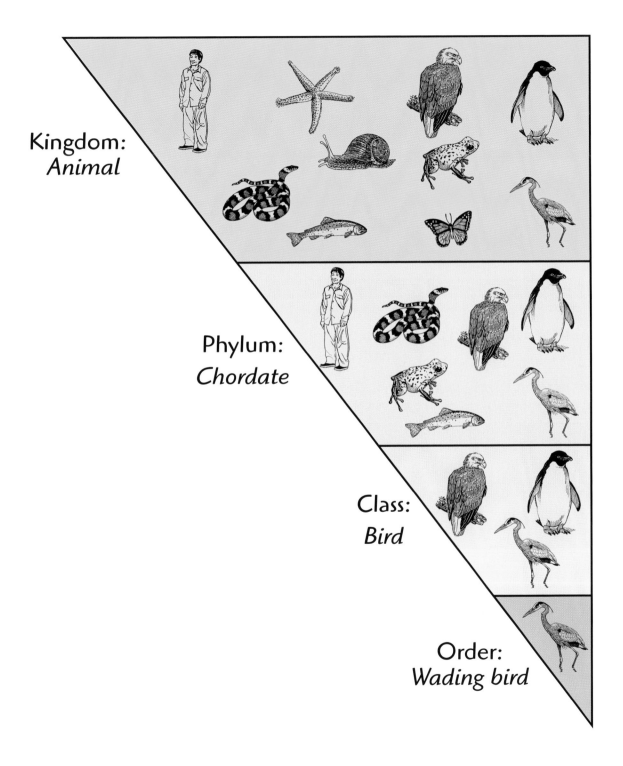

Kingdom: *Animal*

Phylum: *Chordate*

Class: *Bird*

Order: *Wading bird*

11

Herons

FAMILY: Ardeidae
COMMON EXAMPLE: Great blue heron
GENUS AND SPECIES: *Ardea herodias*
HEIGHT: 39 to 52 inches (99 to 132 cm)

Out on a marsh, a great blue heron stands perfectly still as it peers into the water. The bird waits patiently for prey to pass by. When the heron spots a fish or frog, it quickly spears the animal with its long, pointed bill and gulps it down.

Moments later, another great blue heron lands in the marsh. The first heron doesn't welcome intruders! It stands tall and stretches its neck to send a warning. The trespassing heron does not scare easily, though.

The first heron stands even taller. It stretches its long neck up and points its head down. "Rok-rok! Rok-rok!" the bird calls, but the stranger won't leave. The first heron bends its neck and pulls its head back, ready to strike. Then it runs at the intruder, screaming, "Crahnk! Crahnk!" Finally, the stranger gets the message and flies off. No wonder people call the great blue heron "the cranky bird!"

In the spring, great blue herons nest together in big, noisy *rookeries*. The males bring sticks to the females so they can build big platform nests.

During this time, the birds *court* each other. They bend their heads down and raise their tails. Then they stretch their necks up high. Finally, the birds lock the tips of their bills together and sway back and forth. They look as if they are kissing! After the birds mate, the female lays eggs. Soon the herons will have a nest full of young.

Bitterns

FAMILY: Ardeidae
COMMON EXAMPLE: American bittern
GENUS AND SPECIES: *Botaurus lentiginosus*
HEIGHT: 23 to 34 inches (58 to 86 cm)

The American bittern is a secretive bird. It lives alone in salt marshes, hidden among the reeds. If an enemy comes near, a bittern has a good trick. It faces the enemy, stretches its neck up straight, and points its bill skyward. Then the bird sways slowly back and forth, just like the reeds around it. The stripes on the bittern's neck and breast look like reeds too. If the enemy circles the bird, the bittern keeps turning so that its thin, striped breast always faces forward. The enemy doesn't even see it!

A bittern may be hard to see, but it's easy to hear. You can't miss a male's loud calls at breeding time. To attract a female and mark his territory, a male makes a loud pumping sound: "Oong-KA-chunk! Oong-KA-chunk!" The bird can be heard for half a mile! You can understand why people call this bird the "thunder-pumper."

After the birds mate, the female builds a nest on a mat of reeds, cattails, and grasses. Then she lays a few greenish-brown eggs. Like the bird, the nest and eggs blend in with their surroundings.

By the time the young bitterns leave the nest, they have learned their parents' hiding trick. At the first sign of danger, they stretch their sharp, pointed bills at the sky and sway like the reeds.

Ibises

FAMILY: Threskiornithidae
COMMON EXAMPLE: Scarlet ibis
GENUS AND SPECIES: *Eudocimus ruber*
HEIGHT: 24 inches (61 cm)

It's the end of the day in a tropical swamp filled with *mangrove* trees. The dark-leaved bushes look tired and drab. Then, as if by magic, hundreds of bright red scarlet ibises seem to appear out of nowhere and land on the bushes. Suddenly, the bushes look as if they have bloomed with large red flowers. The birds will *roost* here all night long.

Scarlet ibises like company. They roost and nest together in great flocks. Their feathers are such a bright red that it is impossible to miss them!

During the day, scarlet ibises stalk around lagoons and swamps. They probe the muddy water with their long, curving bills. All the while, the birds grunt and babble to one another. When an ibis's bill touches something good to eat, it snaps shut automatically. Then the ibis gulps down its prey.

In the shallow water, ibises find crayfish, crabs, water insects, and snails. Sometimes they eat fish and frogs too. Often, they stalk around in mudflats or wet fields in search of worms and insects. They also find food among the spreading roots of mangrove trees.

What makes these birds so red? The bodies of the crabs and shrimp they eat contain an orange chemical, called *carotene* that colors their feathers. The birds with the reddest feathers have caught the most crabs and shrimp.

Spoonbills

FAMILY: Threskiornithidae
COMMON EXAMPLE: Roseate spoonbill
GENUS AND SPECIES: *Ajaia ajaja*
HEIGHT: 30 to 32 inches (76 to 81 cm)

The roseate spoonbill has beautiful pink, red, and white feathers—and the face of a clown. Its head is naked and greenish, and its bill looks like a long, flat spoon. That odd-looking bill is a great tool, though. As a spoonbill wades through shallow water, it sweeps its partly open bill back and forth under the surface. When the bird feels a tasty critter floating or swimming by, its bill snaps shut. Dinner is served!

A spoonbill finds all kinds of good things to eat that way. It gulps down fish, shrimp, crayfish, crabs, beetles, snails, and slugs. Unlike most other wading birds, a spoonbill sometimes eats the roots and stems of water plants too. Like its relative, the scarlet ibis, the color of a roseate spoonbill's pink feathers comes from a chemical in the shrimp it eats.

Spoonbills are like ibises in another way—they roost and nest in large groups. In the spring, males and females begin to court. They chase after one another for a while, and then they perch next to each other. Soon, they cross their bills and clasp them together. Then they offer each other sticks. The female spoonbill uses the sticks to build a platform nest. Then she lays her eggs and sits on them until they hatch.

18

19

Storks

FAMILY: Ciconiidae
COMMON NAME: Wood stork
GENUS AND SPECIES: *Mycteria americana*
HEIGHT: 40 to 44 inches (100 to 110 cm)

Have you ever watched a wood stork hunting for prey? As the bird wades through a shallow marsh, it holds its bill open under the water and stirs the mud with its feet. When it feels a startled fish with its bill, the bill instantly snaps shut. No other bird has such a fast reaction!

A wood stork has no feathers on its head. If it did, the feathers would get very dirty in the muddy water. Wood storks like fish best, but they also eat crayfish, frogs, snakes, and baby alligators. A wood stork usually eats about 1 pound (0.5 kg) of food a day. During the breeding season, however, wood storks need about 440 pounds (200 kg) of food to feed themselves and their chicks.

Wood storks do not breed until they are 4 years old, but when they do, they mate for life. Colonies of birds build platform nests high in the trees where their young will be safe from most *predators*.

These birds are quiet most of the time, but not when they are near their nests. Then the adults hiss and clap their bills loudly to scare off enemies.

Herons

FAMILY: Ardeidae

COMMON EXAMPLE: Boat-billed heron

GENUS AND SPECIES: *Cochlearius cochlearius*

HEIGHT: 20 inches (51 cm)

It's easy to see how the boat-billed heron got its name. Its bill looks like a boat turned upside down. Like other herons, it wades through the water in search of fish. When it sees a likely meal, the bird stabs the prey with its sharp bill. During the breeding season, the boat-billed heron pokes its bill around in the mud to find prey. With its extra-wide bill, it scoops up shrimp and other small creatures.

Boat-billed herons usually hunt at night. During the day, they rest quietly in thick mangrove thickets and *preen*, or clean and smooth, their feathers. Like other herons, they have patches of special feathers called *powder down*. These feathers are very fragile. When a heron rubs them with its bill, they crumble into a powdery material. The heron then spreads the powder on its feathers to soak up slime from fish and eels. Then it combs out its feathers with its third toe, which has a jagged edge. The bird is fresh and clean again!

Boat-billed herons nest in colonies in the tangled lower branches of mangrove trees. Because these trees have so many branches, the birds cannot see one another easily. When it is time to find a mate and guard their territory, boat-billed herons make noisy popping sounds with their bills. Some people say it sounds as if a crowd of people are clapping their hands.

Herons

FAMILY: Ardeidae
COMMON EXAMPLE: Goliath heron
GENUS AND SPECIES: *Ardea goliath*
HEIGHT: 59 inches (150 cm)

The Goliath heron lives near inland lakes and coastal *estuaries*—places where rivers meet the sea—in the southern part of Africa. If you ever travel to Victoria Falls in the country of Zimbabwe or to the Zambezi River, which flows through several African countries, you might be lucky enough to see a Goliath heron.

Can you guess how this bird got its name? It's really big! A Goliath heron is the tallest and largest heron in the world.

When a Goliath heron hunts, it wades up to its belly in the water. Its long legs let the bird wade deeper than any other heron, so it can find food that other birds can't reach. Sometimes it stands still and peers into the water, looking for fish. When the Goliath spots a tasty treat, it lowers its body and crouches, ready to strike. Then, zap! It straightens its long, curved neck and spears the fish.

At other times, a Goliath heron stalks through mudflats or swamps in search of crabs, frogs, turtles, and small mammals. It even eats baby alligators. A Goliath heron eats whatever comes its way!

Once in a while, a Goliath heron combs powder down through its feathers to clean off the fish slime. This bird also spends time resting on one foot, with the other tucked up in its belly feathers.

Shoebills

FAMILY: Balaenicipitidae
COMMON NAME: Shoebill
GENUS AND SPECIES: *Balaeniceps rex*
HEIGHT: 47 inches (120 cm)

The shoebill's scientific name means "king whalehead." The Arab people who live near the marshes of the upper Nile River, in Africa, gave the bird a name that means "father of the shoe." No matter what name they use, most people would agree this is an odd-looking bird.

Its big bill measures about 9 inches (23 cm) long and 4 inches (10 cm) across. Some people think it looks like an upside-down shoe with a large hook on the end. This bird always looks as if it is smiling at some private joke.

The shoebill looks odd when it flies too. It pulls its head back on its shoulders and flies heavily along with its legs trailing behind. Some people think the crown of raised feathers on top of the shoebill's head looks like a little hat.

The shoebill lives in African wetlands. As it stalks slowly through deep marshes and climbs over floating water plants, it spreads out its weight on its long, thin toes. When the shoebill spots a fish, frog, or snake, it lunges forward, stretches its whole body, and spreads open its huge wings. Its long bill can hold a big, slippery fish with no trouble at all. Most of the time, the shoebill scoops up a bunch of water

plants with its prey. It has to turn its catch over to separate the food from the plants.

A shoebill also uses its bill to dig up lungfish and turtles hiding in the mud. On hot days during the nesting season, the bird fills its bill with water and pours it on young birds to cool them down.

Storks

FAMILY: Ciconiidae
COMMON EXAMPLE: Marabou stork
GENUS AND SPECIES: *Leptoptilos crumeniferus*
HEIGHT: 59 inches (150 cm)

Out on the Serengeti Plain, in East Africa, a small flock of marabou storks circle high in the air. They have just spotted a lion feeding on a zebra. They circle lower and lower, drifting down on air currents while the lion finishes its meal. Finally, it's their turn to eat! They land on the prey and begin fighting over its meat.

A marabou stork is not a pretty bird. It has a pink, naked head with a large *wattle*, or sac of skin, dangling from its neck. Because it feeds on dead bodies, this bird's feathers sometimes get messy.

When it is time to find a mate, a male marabou stork inflates his wattle with air and slowly raises and lowers his head. Then he sways back and forth. All the while, he clacks his bill and makes strange mooing, grunting, and whistling calls.

Large groups of these storks build big stick nests in one area. The males gather the sticks, and the females place them on the nests. When the young hatch, they are helpless, so their parents feed and take care of them. The adult birds spend all their time searching for dead animals on the plains or digging for scraps in garbage dumps. They eat the food and then return to the nest. They throw up the half-digested food and feed it to the hungry chicks.

Hammerkops

FAMILY: Scopidae
COMMON NAME: Hammerkop
GENUS AND SPECIES: *Scopus umbretta*
HEIGHT: 22 inches (56 cm)

The hammerkop is another odd-looking African bird. It has a big tuft of feathers streaming from the back of its hammer-shaped head.

At one time, people in Africa told many stories about the hammerkop. They thought it was a wise and magical creature—a sort of bird witch. They even believed that harming a hammerkop meant bad luck would come. In some areas, if a hammerkop flew over a house, the people moved out. They thought it meant that someone in the house would die.

Hammerkops like company. They often live in groups of eight to twelve birds. At breeding time, the male and female dance, bow to each other, and flap their wings. As they dance, they yap and cackle.

After the birds mate, they build a huge nest between the branches of a tree. The giant nest can be up to 6 feet (2 m) across and so strong that a person can stand on it. It takes the birds 4 to 6 weeks to build their dome-shaped nest out of sticks, mud, and manure. The hammerkops make a tiny entrance hole on one side of the nest. Inside are three "rooms"—a front "hall" that serves as a lookout post, a "living room" for the young, and a nest room.

To get inside the tiny entrance hole, a hammerkop flies straight at it, folds its wings at the last moment, and dives inside. Enemies have a hard time getting into a hammerkop nest.

Storks

FAMILY: Ciconiidae
COMMON EXAMPLE: White stork
GENUS AND SPECIES: *Ciconia ciconia*
HEIGHT: 36 inches (91 cm)

In some parts of the world, white storks are the most familiar wading birds. They often build their nests on rooftops. Many people believe white storks bring good luck. In some small towns, people put platforms on their roofs hoping the storks will nest there. Unfortunately, white storks no longer nest in many of their traditional homes.

In the spring, white storks *migrate* hundreds of miles north from tropical Africa to Europe. They usually go back to the same nest year after year.

A stork has no voice box and cannot call. To get a female's attention at mating time, the male does a special dance, rattling and clattering his long bill. Then he brings sticks to the female, and she uses them to build a bulky nest. When the nest is finished, she lays three to five eggs.

When a male returns to the nest, he has a strange way of greeting his mate. He throws his head back so that it rests upside down on his back and clatters his bill loudly. The female copies him. The birds look as if their necks are broken!

Both parents feed the helpless young. The adult birds swallow insects, frogs, fish, and other small animals they find in marshes and

grasslands. Then they fly back to the nest and throw up partially digested food to feed their hungry chicks.

Flamingos

FAMILY: Phoenicopteridae
COMMON EXAMPLE: Greater flamingo
GENUS AND SPECIES: *Phoenicopterus ruber*
HEIGHT: 57 inches (145 cm)

Have you ever seen a flock of flamingos feed in a saltwater marsh? They walk along slowly with their bills upside down in the water. The birds look as if they are smiling! Inside their bills, hairlike combs called *lamellae* (LAH-mel-ee) strain tiny animals out of the water. A substance in the animals they eat gives flamingos their pink color.

Flamingos enjoy the company of other flamingos. A flock may have thousands of birds. At mating time, all the birds wag their heads, twist and preen, and flash their wings. Then they walk backward and forward together—all marching quickly in step.

Flamingos nest together too. Each pair builds a flat-topped cone of mud to nest in. Then the female lays a single egg in a hole at the top of the nest. Each mound is about two neck-lengths from its neighbors. The birds defend their nests from other flamingos. They spread their wings to make themselves look scary and honk loudly at intruders. A flock of flamingos can be very noisy!

When a flamingo chick hatches, both parents feed it with a red, milky liquid they make in their throats. The young flamingo has a long life to look forward to. It may live up to 30 years.

Egrets

FAMILY: Ardeidae
COMMON EXAMPLE: Cattle egret
GENUS AND SPECIES: *Bubulcus ibis*
HEIGHT: 20 inches (51 cm)

The best place to see cattle egrets is in a field of cows. The cattle move about as they eat the grasses, stirring up insects with their hooves. The cattle egrets strut steadily along behind. When an egret spots an insect, it darts forward and stabs at the prey. If the insect is small, the bird swallows it right down. If the insect is too big to swallow, the egret jabs at it or dips it in water to make it easier to eat.

In different parts of the world, cattle egrets follow different kinds of animals, including buffaloes, rhinos, elephants, zebras, giraffes, and antelopes. In Australia, egrets even follow kangaroos! Sometimes the birds follow a farmer plowing a field and gobble up the worms the plow turns up.

Cattle egrets nest in large colonies with other wading birds. Males carry sticks to the females, who build the nests. Sometimes males steal sticks from other birds' nests. Females lay three or four eggs. For 24 days, males and females take turns sitting on the eggs.

After the young egrets hatch, the adults spread their wings over the chicks' heads to protect them from the hot sun. For about 6 weeks, the parents spend most of their time hunting. They keep the prey in special throat pouches and bring it back to the nest to feed their chicks.

Herons

FAMILY: Ardeidae
COMMON EXAMPLE: Black-crowned night heron
GENUS AND SPECIES: *Nycticorax nycticorax*
HEIGHT: 23 to 28 inches (58 to 71 cm)

As night falls in a woodland swamp, a black-crowned night heron crouches on a stump, waiting for total darkness. After a while, the bird flies down and begins stalking slowly through the swamp. As the heron walks, its bill *vibrates* in the water. Soon a fish swims up to investigate. Snap! The heron grabs the prey and swallows it whole.

During the day, black-crowned night herons roost quietly in the trees. At night, though, people can often hear their loud "Quark! Quark!" Sometime people call these birds "night ravens" because of the harsh noises they make.

Black-crowned night herons eat crayfish, mussels, squid, snakes, frogs, and anything else they happen to spot. Sometimes they eat dead animals and garbage from dumps.

Most of the time, night herons have yellow-green legs. But if you see one with red legs, you'll know it is mating season. During this time, the males dance for the females, snap their bills, hiss, and shake twigs. The females seem to enjoy the show! Soon the males and females mate and the females lay their eggs. Then the birds raise their families in big stick nests.

If you ever come across a colony of nesting black-crowned night herons, try not to disturb them. The chicks may lean out of the nest and throw up on you!

Egrets

FAMILY: Ardeidae

COMMON EXAMPLE: Great egret

GENUS AND SPECIES: *Casmerodius albus*

HEIGHT: 35 to 41 inches (89 to 104 cm)

It is breeding time out on the sandbar. The male great egrets have begun courting the females. They gurgle and strut about to show off their beautiful white tail *plumes*.

Suddenly, two males face each other—plumes erect. One stabs his beak at his rival. The other bird jerks his head and then strikes back. The first male dodges and strikes again. This battle goes on until one of the birds gives up. Then the males begin dancing around the females again. After the birds mate, they build nest platforms high in the treetops. Most of the time, they choose nest sites near other colonies of wading birds.

The male and female take turns sitting on the eggs. When it's time for the "changing of the guard," the birds perform a little ritual. The male lands on a nearby branch and squawks hoarsely. Then he raises his wings and walks along the branch toward his mate, with his plumes floating out behind him. The female answers by raising her head and spreading her own plumes. Finally, she flies off, and the male settles down on the eggs.

The great egret's beautiful plumes nearly became its downfall. In the past, hunters killed egrets so that they could sell the plumes to

people who made women's hats. Just in time, people passed laws to protect these beautiful birds. Today, their numbers are increasing.

Wading Birds and People

About 100 years ago, fashionable women liked to wear hats with feathers. Many snowy egrets, roseate spoonbills, scarlet ibises, and other wading birds with beautiful plumes were killed for their feathers. At that time, 1 ounce (28 g) of egret feathers was worth almost twice as much as 1 ounce (28 g) of gold! Some people also killed flamingos and herons for food.

Today there are laws protecting all these birds. Killing them is illegal. Even if you find a

This woman is very proud of her showy hat.

feather from one of these birds on the ground, you need a special permit to keep it. Thanks to these laws, the number of egrets, spoonbills, ibises, and flamingos is slowly increasing.

In the 1960s, scientists noticed that the number of fish-eating birds was dropping. When they tried to find out why, they learned that many of their eggs broke before the chicks were ready to hatch.

Why were the eggshells so thin and delicate? The problem was caused by a poisonous chemical called *DDT* that people sprayed on swamps to kill mosquitoes. When fish ate the mosquitoes, DDT ended up in their bodies. Then, birds ate the fish, and the poison ended up in their bodies too. Because birds eat a lot of fish, large amounts of DDT built up inside them. One result of all that poison was that the female birds produced eggs with thinner shells.

Wading birds face other problems too. When people destroy the places where birds live to make room for buildings and parking lots, the birds lose their homes. They have nowhere to build nests, lay eggs, raise young, and hunt for food. In addition, water pollution and acid rain often kill the fish and frogs that wading birds eat. American bitterns, night herons, and wood storks are now in danger of disappearing from Earth forever, but if people work hard to protect them and their habitats, these wonderful birds may be able to survive.

An American bittern

Words to Know

carotene—an orange substance found in some plants and animals

class—a group of creatures within a phylum that share certain characteristics

colony—a large group of animals, such as birds, that live and nest together

court—to try to attract a mate

DDT—a poison once used to kill pests and later found to be harmful to many animals. It is now illegal in some countries, including the United States.

estuary—a wide part of a river where it meets the sea

family—a group of creatures within an order that share certain characteristics

genus (plural **genera**)—a group of creatures within a family that share certain characteristics

kingdom—one of the five divisions into which all living things are placed: the animal kingdom, the plant kingdom, the fungus kingdom, the moneran kingdom, and the protist kingdom

lamella (plural **lamellae**)—hairlike combs on the inside of some birds' bills used for straining food from the water

mangrove—a small, shrubby tree that has many roots and grows in parts of the world that are warm all year long

migrate—to travel from one place to another to find food or have young

order—a group of creatures within a class that share certain characteristics

phylum (plural **phyla**)—a group of creatures within a kingdom that share certain characteristics

plume—a large, distinctive feather

powder down—a patch of small, crumbly feathers that some wading birds use to clean themselves

predator—an animal that hunts and eats other animals

preen—to smooth and clean feathers or fur

prey—an animal that is hunted and eaten by other animals

rookery—a place where birds build nests, lay eggs, and raise their young

roost—to settle somewhere for the night

species—a group of creatures within a genus that share certain characteristics. Members of a species can mate and produce young

wattle—a wrinkled fold or sac of skin that hangs from the neck of some birds

vibrate—to move quickly back and forth

Learning More

Books

Garcia, Eulalia, et al. *Storks: Majestic Migrators*. Milwaukee, WI: Gareth Stevens, 1996.

Jewet, Sarah Orne. *A White Heron*. Cambridge, MA: Candlewick, 1997.

McMillan, Bruce. *Wild Flamingos*. Boston: Houghton Mifflin Company, 1997.

Peterson, Roger Tory. *Peterson's First Guide to the Birds*. Minneapolis, MN: Lerner, 1997.

Rupp, Rebecca, and Jeffrey C. Domm. *Everything You Never Learned About Birds: Lore & Legends*. Pownal, VT: Storey Publishing, 1995.

Web Sites

Cornell Laboratory of Ornithology

http://www.ornith.cornell.edu

This site lets students participate in an online BirdWatch project. It also features a bird of the week, other bird projects, and information about how people can help protect the world's birds.

Peterson Online

http://www.petersononline.com/birds/

This site offers a tutorial, Peterson's Perspective, to help beginning birders learn about birding and birds. The site includes links to other birding pages, recommended reading, calendars, and more.

The Virtual Birder

http://www.virtualbirder.com

This site has something for everyone interested in birds, including pictures of rare birds, links to other birding sites on the Web, virtual tours, tips on how to find birds in your area, and much more.

Index

About the Author

Sara Swan Miller has enjoyed working with children all her life, first as a Montessori nursery-school teacher and later as an outdoor environmental educator at the Mohonk Preserve in New Paltz, New York. As the director of the preserve's school program, she has led hundreds of children on field trips and taught them the importance of appreciating and respecting the natural world.

Miller has written a number of children's books, including *Three Stories You Can Read to Your Cat*; *Three Stories You Can Read to Your Dog*; *Three More Stories You Can Read to Your Dog*; *What's in the Woods?: An Outdoor Activity Book*; *Oh, Cats of Camp Rabbitbone*; *Piggy in the Parlor and Other Tales*; *Better Than TV*; and *Will You Sting Me? Will You Bite?: The Truth About Some Scary-Looking Insects*. She has also written five books about farm animals for Children's Press's True Books series and several other books for the Animals in Order series.

13